NAIL ARTISTRY

Creative Designs and Techniques for Beautiful Nails

MYLA BUSH

TABLE CONTENTS

History

Nail polish (also known as nail varnish or nail enamel) is a lacquer that can be applied to the human fingernail or toenails to decorate and protect the nail plates. The formula has been revised repeatedly to enhance its decorative properties and to suppress cracking or peeling. Nail polish consists of a mix of an organic polymer and several other components that give it colors and textures. Nail polishes come in all color shades and play a significant part in manicures and pedicures.

Thousands of years ago, women and men began decorating their nails not only for beauty but as a class distinction. The earliest instance of colored nails was in 3200 B.C. when males in Babylon dyed their nails with kohl before going into battle. During 3000 B.C., the Chinese and Egyptians used beeswax, egg whites, gelatin, natural gums and flowers to make nail colors. Around 600 B.C., the lower class in China was sentenced to death for wearing nail polish, while the royal echelons preferred metallic, gold and silver. Henna was used in Egypt, as evidenced by the mummified pharaohs. The use of henna may have started in India during the Bronze Age before the Chinese improved upon it to achieve limited color choices.

When the automobile industry used pigments of various colors suspended in a solvent-borne coating during the 20th century, the polish of the old autocracy evolved to become nail polishes requiring an hour or more to dry which then chipped after a few days. We will refer to these compositions as "traditional nail polish' consisting of:

A film-forming polymer called nitrocellulose, a member of the gun cotton family.
Volatile organic solvents such as butyl acetate, ethyl acetate, and toluene. Most companies have now reformulated out toluene in their products.

Plasticizers to prevent the film former from becoming brittle such as tribute citrate, camphor, DBP, and TPHP. Most companies have replaced the last three.

Resins to modify the properties of the nitrocellulose such as tosylamide/formaldehyde and tosylamide/epoxy resins.

Pigments: The U.S. FDA approves only colorants that are FDC-certified.

Thickening agents to keep the pigments suspended, of which the most common are modified clays such as stearalkonium hectorite and stearalkonium bentonite.

Ultraviolet (UV) stabilizers to delay the bleaching of the colors in sunlight. Benzophenone-1 is the most common.

Modern nail professionals routinely apply traditional nail polish over a base coat and then finish with a top coat. The purpose of the base coat is to improve the adhesion of the polish to the nail surface and prevent its pigments from staining the natural nail. The top coat is then applied over the nail polish to create a glossier finish while resisting abrasion.

Before the 1960s, traditional nail polishes were only applied directly to bare nails, and convention clearly defined that all manicures and pedicures were services intended for natural nails. Women loved the availability of numerous colors and their fancy names but wished for instant long nails and fast-drying, long-wearing polish on natural nails.

Product developers delivered on these desires with the advent of new technologies. It all began in 1954, when Dr. Fred Slack, a dentist, broke his fingernail and mended it using dental materials. Other companies ultimately advanced his invention, which became known as artificial nails or acrylic nail enhancements. Acrylic nail enhancements provided instantly long nails and solved the premature chipping issues of traditional nail polish because the acrylic surface provided a uniform composition resulting in a predictable adhesion.

In 1982, UV lamps were first used in nail services with the introduction of hard gels by James Giuliano. These high-viscosity liquid formulations are supplied in jars, brushed onto the natural nail, and hardened (or cured) when exposed to UV light. They're called hard gels because of their abrasion resistance, and once cured, the only way to remove them is by filing them off.

In 1990, I invented the first UV top coat. It was formulated to effectively dry freshly applied traditional nail polish when allowed to air-dry for three minutes, then exposed to UV light for three to four minutes.

Traditional nail polish was the only product available to impart color to acrylic, gel and natural nails until the 21st century.

The first long-wear polish was introduced in 2007. These products are like traditional nail polish; however, there is no curing involved, wears like gel polish (that came later) and is removed by wiping off with regular nail polish removers. Long-wear polish's no yellowing property uniquely stands out due to the absence of nitrocellulose. Unlike traditional polishes, which may take 60 minutes or more to dry, this long-wear polish air-dries fully in just five minutes and provides a seven-to-14-day chip-free wear like a gel.

Other modern innovations brought colored acrylics and UV gel polishes, introduced in 2009, and Shellac™ in 2010. UV gel polishes, supplied in a bottle with a brush, are modified UV hard gel with traditional polish in one formulation, resulting in a colored gel that can be removed by filing off or soaking the cured coating in pure acetone. Hybrids, introduced in 2013, cure in sunlight and have a higher ratio of polish components to gel, making them easier to remove than gel polishes.

Modern innovations also include dip systems, which like acrylics, are two-component liquid and powder systems that use the same removal methods but differ in curing chemistries. And finally, press-on nails and polish strips were introduced as solvent-free and instant-dry options.

All products described above are applied to natural nails, exposing the nail surface when the wearer removes the coating. They differ from each other by their permanency or degree of attachment to the natural nail.

What motivating factors led to these historic innovations within the nail polish industry?

Convenience
Time savings
Longevity of wear
Wellness awareness
Currently, trending innovations include "manicure robots" in response to a shortage of professional nail technicians. Of course, no machine will ever replicate our many human innovators and artists' pure passion, vision or talents. Those who have forged this illustrious history for centuries will pass on the legacy for generations to come. Our future is bright.

Ingredients

Modern nail polish consists predominately of a film-forming polymer dissolved in a volatile organic solvent. The most common polymer is nitrocellulose, although the more expensive cellulose acetates such as CAB are claimed to give better performance. In gel nail varnish the polymer is usually some sort of acrylate copolymer. The solvents are commonly butyl acetate or ethyl acetate. Low levels of various additives are included to give the desired finish:

- Plasticizers to yield non-brittle films. diethyl phthalate, dibutylphthalate and camphor are typical.
- Dyes and pigments. Representative compounds include chromium oxide greens, chromium hydroxide, ferric Ferro cyanide, stannic oxide, titanium dioxide, iron oxide, carmine, ultramarine, and manganese violet.
- Opalescent pigments. The glittery/shimmer look in the color can be conferred by mica, bismuth oxychloride, natural pearls, and aluminum powder.
- Adhesive polymers ensure that the nitrocellulose adheres to the nail's surface. One modifier used is tosylamide-formaldehyde resin.
- Thickening agents are added to maintain the sparkling particles in suspension while in the bottle. A typical thickener is stearalkonium hectoliter. Thickening agents exhibit thixotropic, their solutions are viscous when still but free-flowing when agitated. This duality is convenient for easily applying the freshly shaken mixture to give a film that quickly rigidifies.
- Ultraviolet stabilizers resist color changes when the dry film is exposed to sunlight. A typical stabilizer is benzophenone-1.

There is no single formula for nail polish. There are, however, a number of ingredient types that are used. These basic components include: film forming agents, resins and plasticizers, solvents, and coloring agents. The exact formulation of a nail polish, apart from being a corporate secret, greatly depends upon choices made by chemists and chemical engineers in the research and development phase of manufacturing. Additionally, as chemicals and other ingredients become accepted or discredited for some uses, adjustments are made. For example, formaldehyde was once frequently used in polish production, but now it is rarely used.

The primary ingredient in nail polish is nitrocellulose (cellulose nitrate) cotton, a flammable and explosive ingredient also used in making dynamite. Nitrocellulose is a liquid mixed with tiny, near-microscopic cotton fibers. In the manufacturing process, the cotton fibers are ground even smaller and do not need to be removed. The nitrocellulose can be purchased in various viscosities to match the desired viscosity of the final product.

Nitrocellulose acts as a film forming agent. For nail polish to work properly, a hard film must form on the exposed surface of the nail, but it cannot form so quickly that it prevents the material underneath from drying. (Consider commercial puddings or gelatin products that dry or film on an exposed surface and protect the moist product underneath.) By itself or used with other functional ingredients, the nitrocellulose film is brittle and adheres poorly to nails.

Manufacturers add synthetic resins and plasticizers (and occasionally similar, natural products) to their mixes to improve flexibility, resistance to soap and water, and other qualities; older recipes sometimes even used nylon for this purpose. Because of the number of desired qualities involved, however, there is no single resin or combination of resins that meets every specification. Among the resins and plasticizers in use today are castor oil, amyl and butyl stearate, and mixes of glycerol, fatty acids, and acetic acids.

The colorings and other components of nail polish must be contained within one or more solvents that hold the colorings and other materials until the polish is applied. After application, the solvent must be able to evaporate. In many cases, the solvent also acts a plasticizer. Butyl stearate and acetate compounds are perhaps the most common.

Finally, the polish must have a color. Early polishes used soluble dyes, but today's product contains pigments of one type or another. Choice of pigment and its ability to mix well with the solvent and other ingredients is essential to producing a good quality product.

Nail polish is a "suspension" product, in which particles of color can only be held by the solvent for a relatively short period of time, rarely more than two or three years. Shaking a bottle of nail polish before use helps to restore settled particles to the suspension; a very old bottle of nail polish may have so much settled pigment that it can never be restored to the solvent. The problem of settling is perhaps the most difficult to be addressed in the manufacturing process.

Manufacturers add synthetic resins and plasticizers (and occasionally similar, natural products) to their mixes to improve flexibility, resistance to soap and water, and other qualities; older recipes sometimes even used nylon for this purpose. Because of the number of desired qualities involved, however, there is no single resin or combination of resins that meets every specification. Among the resins and plasticizers in use today are castor oil, amyl and butyl stearate, and mixes of glycerol, fatty acids, and acetic acids.

The colorings and other components of nail polish must be contained within one or more solvents that hold the colorings and other materials until the polish is applied. After application, the solvent must be able to evaporate. In many cases, the solvent also acts a plasticizer. Butyl stearate and acetate compounds are perhaps the most common.

Finally, the polish must have a color. Early polishes used soluble dyes, but today's product contains pigments of one type or another. Choice of pigment and its ability to mix well with the solvent and other ingredients is essential to producing a good quality product.

Nail polish is a "suspension" product, in which particles of color can only be held by the solvent for a relatively short period of time, rarely more than two or three years. Shaking a bottle of nail polish before use helps to restore settled particles to the suspension; a very old bottle of nail polish may have so much settled pigment that it can never be restored to the solvent. The problem of settling is perhaps the most difficult to be addressed in the manufacturing process.

The Manufacturing Process

Early methods of making nail polish used a variety of methods that today look charmingly amateurish. One common technique was to mix cleaned scraps of movie film and other cellulose with alcohol and castor oil and leave the mixture to soak overnight in a covered container. The mixture was then strained, colored, and perfumed. Though recognizable as nail polish, the product was far from what we have available today.

The modern manufacturing process is a very sophisticated operation utilizing highly skilled workers, advanced machinery, and even robotics. Today's consumers expect a nail polish to apply smoothly, evenly, and easily; to set relatively quickly; and to be resistant to chipping and peeling. In addition, the polish should be dermatologically innocuous.

Mixing the pigment with nitrocellulose and plasticizer

1 The pigments are mixed with nitrocellulose and plasticizer using a "two-roll" differential speed mill. This mill grinds the pigment between a pair of rollers that are able to work with increasing speed as the pigment is ground down. The goal is to produce fine dispersion of the color. A variation of this mill is the Banbury Mixer (used also in the production of rubber for rubber bands).

2 When properly and fully milled, the mixture is removed from the mill in sheet form and then broken up into small chips for mixing with the solvent. The mixing is performed in stainless steel kettles that can hold anywhere from 5 to 2,000 gallons. Stainless steel must be used because the nitrocellulose is extremely reactive in the presence of iron. The kettles are jacketed so that the mixture can be cooled by circulating cold water or another liquid around the outside of the kettle. The temperature of the kettle, and the rate of cooling, are controlled by both computers and technicians.

This step is performed in a special room or area designed to control the hazards of fire and explosion. Most modern factories perform this step in an area with walls that will close in if an alarm sounds and, in the event of explosion, with ceilings that will safely blow off without endangering the rest of the structure.

Adding other ingredients

3 Materials are mixed in computerized, closed kettles. At the end of the process, the mix is cooled slightly before the addition of such other materials as perfumes and moisturizers.

4 The mixture is then pumped into smaller, 55 gallon drums, and then trucked to a production line. The finished nail polish is pumped into explosion proof pumps, and then into smaller bottles suitable for the retail market.

Quality Control

Extreme attention to quality control is essential throughout the manufacturing process. Not only does quality control increase safety in the process, but it is the only way that a manufacturer can be assured of consumer confidence and loyalty. A single bottle of poor quality polish can lose a customer forever. Regardless of quality control, however, no single nail polish is perfect; the polish always represents a chemical compromise between what is desired and what the manufacturer is able to produce.

The nail polish is tested throughout the manufacturing process for several important factors (drying time, smoothness of flow, gloss, hardness, color, abrasion resistance, etc.). Subjective testing, where the mixture or final product is examined or applied, is ongoing. Objective, laboratory testing of samples, though more time consuming, is also necessary to ensure a usable product. Laboratory tests are both complicated and unforgiving, but no manufacturer would do without them.

The Future

Perhaps the major problem with nail polishes—from the consumer's point of view—is the length of the drying time. Various methods of producing fast-drying polish have recently been patented, and these methods, along with others that are still being developed, may result in marketable products. Of all the different types of cosmetics, nail polish is the one that is most likely to continue to be positively affected by advancements and developments in the chemistry field.

Types of nail polish

Base coat

This type of nail polish is a clear, milky-colored, or opaque pink polish formula that is used specifically before applying nail polish to the nail. Its function is to strengthen nails, restore moisture to the nail, and help polish adhere to the nail. It prevents staining and extends the lifespan of the manicure. Some base coats are marketed as "ridge fillers", and can create a smooth surface, de-emphasizing the ridges that can appear on unruffled nails. Some base coats, called "peel off base coats", allow the user to peel off their nail polish without using a remover.

Top coat

This type of nail polish is a clear colored polish formula that is used specifically after applying nail polish to the nail. It forms a hardened barrier for the nail that can prevent chipping, scratching and peeling. Many topcoats are marketed as "quick-drying." Topcoats can help the underlying colored polish dry quickly as well. It gives the polish a more finished and desired look and may help to keep the polish on longer.

Gel

Gel polish is a long-lasting variety of nail polish made up of a type of methacrylate polymer. It is painted on the nail similar to traditional nail polish, but does not dry. Instead it is cured under an ultraviolet lamp or ultraviolet LED. While regular nail polish formulas typically last two to seven days without chipping, gel polish can last as long as two weeks with proper application and home care. Gel polish can be more difficult to remove than regular nail polish. It is usually removed by soaking the nails in pure acetone (the solvent used in most nail polish removers) for five to fifteen minutes, depending on the formula.

Matte

Matte nails create a smooth finish, with no shine. Nail expert and manicurist Roxanne Campbell explains: 'Matte varnishes can even cover imperfections and are becoming popular with my clients. ' She also mentions that matte nails tend to give more of flat, frosted finish, which is perfect for colder months.

Shellac

Shellac polishes mix two types of nail coating: gel (for durability and nail protection) and traditional nail polish (for color and shine). Shellac is thinner and softer than gel polish, but harder than traditional varnish.

Nail polish remover

Nail polish remover is an organic solvent that may also include oils, scents, and coloring. Nail polish remover packages may include individual felt pads soaked in remover, a bottle of liquid remover used with a cotton ball or cotton pad, or a foam-filled container into which one inserts a finger and twists it until the polish comes off. The choice of remover type depends on the user's preference, and often the price or quality of the remover.

The most common remover is acetone. Acetone can also remove artificial nails made of acrylic or cured gel.

An alternative nail polish remover is ethyl acetate, which often also contains isopropyl alcohol. Ethyl acetate is usually the original solvent for nail polish itself.

Acetonitrile has been used as a nail polish remover, but it is more toxic than the aforementioned options. It has been banned in the European Economic Area for use in cosmetics since 17 March 2000.

The Advantages and Disadvantages of Nail Art

Nail art has become very popular nowadays and many women and girls consider already tried or consider having it done. From trendsetters to celebrities many seem sporting fingernail art. It can be an intricate embellished nail or a cool graphic pattern to match the outfit. Having healthy, beautiful and trendy nails can bring more self confidence and can be an ego boost for any woman. There are a great variety of nail art patterns to choose from. If you didn't try nail art yet, then let's analyze together some advantages and disadvantages of this fashionable trend in nail polish.

Nail art Advantages
Nail art offers a great variety of palette colors and you can choose your favorites to raise your mood, to match your lifestyle, your personality and your outfit. A multicolor nail art can cheer you up at any moment. If you are bored of neutral colored nail polish, then a bold graphic or a colored patterned nail art adds some fun.
Nail art is easy to be done.
Focusing on yourself and taking time out from the world can have a therapeutic effect. Setting time aside to work on your nail art is soothing and relaxing. You will also get an ego boost feeling from wearing an impressive nail art pattern.
Nail art gives you an inexpensive way to wear some designer labels.
If you need some creative outlet with your day to day looks, then bold makeup looks are not always a good option. Your nails are perfect canvas and the nail art can be a more convenient way of wearing something creative.
Nail art is fashionable and everyone else seems to wear it. If you want to look cool in a fast and easy way than you just have some nail art done to get yourself on the trend.

Nail art Disadvantages

Some nail art polish can take a long drying time.

Your nail polish may contain too many chemicals and those bright colors may have a bad effect on the nails.

It's not easy to keep the nail polish from getting on your cuticles. Polishing your nails perfectly with a complicated nail art pattern may get some time. Not every woman has the patience to wait calm and without rushing until her manicure is done. Spending hours with nail art isn't an option for most of the women because it's difficult to fit their busy schedule.

The fact that everyone else seems to wear nail art is a double edged sword. On one side, if you choose to wear nail art you'll keep with the trend, on the other side your nail art might get lost in a pool of pretty similar patterns. Try to be as creative as possible when you choose your nail art.

Nail art is hard to perfect and if you have perfectionist tendency it might disappoint you. The slightest crack or smudge can ruin your manicure. When you get into nail art, nail care becomes even more important. Because your nails are the canvas for your pieces of art you need to spend more time and pay more attention to your nail care.

Health and Environmental concerns

1/ Health concerns

The health risks associated with nail polish are disputed. According to the U.S. Department of Health and Human Services, "The amount of chemicals used in animal studies is probably a couple of hundred times higher than what you would be exposed to from using nail polish every week or so. So the chances of any individual phthalate producing such harm [in humans] is very slim." A more serious health risk is faced by professional nail technicians, who perform manicures over a workstation, known as a nail table, on which the client's hands rest – directly below the technician's breathing zone. In 2009, Susan Reutman, an epidemiologist with the U.S. National Institute for Occupational Safety and Health's Division of Applied Research and Technology, announced a federal effort to evaluate the effectiveness of downdraft vented nail tables (VNTs) in removing potential nail polish chemical and dust exposures from the technician's work area. These ventilation systems have potential to reduce worker exposure to chemicals by at least 50%. Many nail technicians will often wear masks to cover their mouth and nose from inhaling any of the harsh dust or chemicals from the nail products.

According to Reutman, a growing body of scientific literature suggests that some inhaled and absorbed organic solvents found in nail salons such as glycol ethers and carbon disulfide may have adverse effects on reproductive health. These effects may be including birth defects, low birth weight, miscarriage, and preterm birth.

Nail polish formulations may include ingredients that are toxic or affect other health problems. One controversial family of ingredient are phthalates, which are implicated as endocrine disruptors and linked to problems in the endocrine system and increased risk of diabetes. Manufacturers have been pressured by consumer groups to reduce or to eliminate potentially-toxic ingredients, and in September 2006, several companies agreed to phase out dibutyl phthalates. There are no universal consumer safety standards for nail polish, however, and while formaldehyde has been eliminated from some nail polish brands, others still use it.

Traditional nail polish

Classic nail polish is painted onto the nail plate, usually in multiple coats, and then air-dried. Conventional nail polish is a polymer dissolved in a solvent. During the drying process, the solvent evaporates, and the polymer hardens. "Hybrid" polish is similar; it is applied and removed the same way as regular polish, but is intended to be longer-lasting.

Pros:
Quickly and easily removed with an acetone-based nail polish remover. Because acetone can be harsh, drying, and damaging, less contact time may mean less damage to the nail plate, skin, and cuticles.
Cons:
Some colors, especially darker colors, can cause nonpermanent discoloration of the nails.

"Non-toxic" nail polish

When it comes to cosmetics, the term "non-toxic" can be difficult to decipher. With regard to nail polish, a commonly used term is "five-free." Five-free refers to polishes that do not contain five specific ingredients: formaldehyde, toluene, dibutyl phthalate, formaldehyde resin, and camphor. There are also brands that market themselves as being free of more substances, such as 7-free or 10-free.

Formaldehyde is a preservative that has been recognized by the National Cancer Institute as a potential cancer-causing substance. It is also among the most common substances that cause allergic contact dermatitis. Formaldehyde resin, dibutyl phthalate, and toluene can also cause allergic contact dermatitis. Camphor is an oil that has been long used as a topical remedy for various conditions, but can be toxic if consumed by mouth.

Studies have shown that chemicals in nail polish can be absorbed into the body. But the exact amount of absorption, and whether it is enough to have negative health effects, are not well established. In general, the question of whether "natural" cosmetic products are safer and healthier still remains, as discussed in an editorial published in JAMA Dermatology.

Pros:
easy removal process akin to regular polish
contains fewer chemicals that can cause contact dermatitis; may be a good option for those with sensitive skin.

Cons:

There is no strong research data regarding whether the chemicals excluded from non-toxic polishes have harmful health effects at the concentrations present in traditional nail polish.
The verdict: This may be a good alternative to conventional polish for those wishing to avoid those particular chemicals, although the health benefits are uncertain.

Gel polish

Gel polish is painted on and then "cured" under a lamp, which dries and hardens the polish almost instantly. Curing of nail polish means photo polymerization, which is a process during which a liquid absorbs energy from UV or visible light and undergoes cross-linking to become a solid. Most curing lamps emit ultraviolet A light, which is a known cause of cellular damage and aging and increases risk of skin cancer. There are some alternative lamps available that emit LED light; however, they may still emit some UV light.

Pros: longer lasting

Cons:
exposure to UV light
Removal process of gel polish can be destructive to nails. Removal involves soaking in acetone, and aggressive buffing, scraping, and peeling of polish, which can injure the nail plate.
Wearing gel polish for long periods may result in severe brittleness and dryness of the nails.

Gel polish is unlikely to have long-term negative effects on nail health if used sporadically or for special occasions. Remind your nail technician to avoid aggressive buffing (always avoid electric buffing), and not to scrape the nail plate forcefully. Never peel or pick off gel polish; doing so may peel off layers of the nail plate along with the polish, resulting in brittleness. Apply sunscreen 20 minutes prior to the UV treatment, or wear fingerless gloves while under the lamp.

Powder dip polish

This manicure entails application of a bonding polish (composed of a resin that is often made up of chemicals used in superglue) that serves as an adhesive for the polish. Next, a finely milled acrylic powder is applied, either by dipping the nail into the powder or brushing it onto the nail. Finally, an activator is applied. This is a liquid containing chemicals that induce polymerization of the resin-containing bonding polish, leaving a hard shell.

Pros: No drying lamp needed, therefore no UV exposure.

Cons:
Sanitation is the major potential issue here. Communal jars of powder may be used for multiple people, which could become a reservoir for bacteria, fungi, and viruses.
Harsh removal process similar to that of gel, often with use of an electric file, can damage the nail plate and cuticle.

Unless a salon is transferring the powder into smaller, individual containers for each client, or using a clean brush to apply the powder, we recommend avoiding this type of manicure.

2/ Regulation and environmental concerns
The U.S. city of San Francisco enacted a city ordinance, publicly identifying establishments that use nail polishes free of the "toxic trio" of dibutyl phthalate, toluene, and formaldehyde.
Nail polish is considered a hazardous waste by some regulatory bodies such as the Los Angeles Department of Public Works. Many countries have strict restrictions on sending nail polish by mail. The "toxic trio" are currently being phased out, but there are still components of nail polish that could cause environmental concern. Leaking out of the bottle into the soil could cause contamination in ground water. Chromium(III) oxide green and Prussian blue are common in nail polish and have shown evidence of going through chemical degradation, which could have a detrimental effect on health.

In fashion

Traditionally, nail polish started in clear, white, red, pink, purple, and black. Nail polish can be found in a diverse variety of colors and shades. Beyond solid colors, nail polish has also developed an array of other designs, such as crackled, glitter, flake, speckled, iridescent, and holographic. Rhinestones or other decorative art are also often applied to nail polish. Some polish is advertised to induce nail growth, make nails stronger, prevent nails from breaking, cracking, or splitting, and even to stop nail biting.

French manicure

French manicures are designed to resemble natural nails, and are characterized by natural pink base nails with white tips. French manicures were one of the first popular and well-known color schemes. French manicures may have originated in the eighteenth-century in Paris but were most popular in the 1920s and 1930s. However, the traditional French manicures were much different from what we know today. They were generally red, while leaving a round crescent shape at the area near the cuticle blank to enhance the lunula of the nail, known now as a half-moon manicure.

With the modern French manicure, trends involving painting different colors for the tips of the nails instead of the white. French tip nails can be made with stickers and stencils. It is still typically done by hand through painting with polish or gel, or sculptured with acrylic.

Social media

Social media has given rise to a nail art culture that allows users to share pictures of their nail art. Women's Wear Daily reports nail polish sales hit a record US$768 million in the United States in 2012, a 32% gain over 2011. Several new polishes and related products came on to the market in the second decade of the twenty-first century as part of the explosion of nail art, such as nail stickers (either made of nail polish or plastic), stencils, magnetic nail polish, nail pens, glitter and sequin topcoats, nail caviar (micro beads), nail polish marketed for men, scented nail polish, and color changing nail polish (some which change hue when exposed to sunshine, and ranges which change hue in response to heat).

Western world

Nail polish in the Western world was more frequently worn by women, going in and out of acceptability depending upon moral customs of the day. In Victorian era culture it was generally considered improper for women to adorn themselves with either makeup or nail coloring, since natural appearances were considered more chaste and pure. In the 1920s, however, women began to wear color in new makeups and nail products, partly in rebellion to such prim customs of their recent past. Since the 1920s, nail colors progressed from French manicures and standard reds to various palettes of color choices, usually coordinated with the fashion industry's clothing colors for the season. By the 1940s the whole nail was painted; before that, it was fashionable to leave the tips and a half-moon on the nail bed bare.

There are 17 principal nail polish finishes:
- Shimmer
- Micro-shimmer
- Micro-glitter
- Glitter
- Frost
- Lustre
- Creme
- Iridescent
- Opalescent

- Matte
- Duochrome
- Jelly or translucent
- Magnetic
- Crackled
- Glass-flecked
- Holographic
- Prismatic micro-glitter or shimmer

The 10 Nail Polish Brands

- Essie
- Chanel
- Lights Lacquer
- CND
- KBShimmer
- OPI
- Tenoverten
- Zoya
- Deborah Lippmann
- Olive and June

Nail Structure and Function

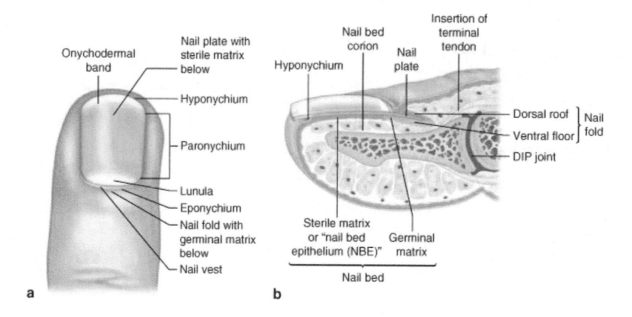

The nail has many soft tissue structures that help support and form the hard-outer nail, known as the nail plate. The attached figure depicts the gross structures described below.

Nail Folds

The nail folds are soft tissue structures that protect the lateral and proximal edges of the nail plate. The proximal nail fold protects most of the nail matrix from trauma and ultraviolet rays.

Mantle

The mantle is the skin covering the matrix and base of the nail plate.

Cuticle

The cuticle (also known as the eponychium) grows from the proximal nail bed and adheres to the nail plate. Together, the proximal nail fold and cuticle form a protective seal against any irritants that may disrupt the matrix underneath.

Nail Matrix

The nail matrix is located deep to the proximal nail fold and nail plate. The proximal nail matrix begins about halfway between the distal interphalangeal joint and the proximal nail fold. The distal nail matrix is visible through the nail plate as a white half-moon structure called the lunular. The nail matrix is responsible for the formation of the hard nail plate and is the only part of the nail unit that contains melanocytes. The nail cells, termed onychocytes, are pushed superficially and distally to form the nail plate. Different parts of the nail matrix form different sections of the nail plate. Generally, the dorsal aspect of the nail plate is formed from the proximal nail matrix, and the ventral nail plate is formed from the distal nail matrix. However, 80% of the nail plate is made from the proximal nail matrix. Therefore, a biopsy or surgery of the distal nail matrix will produce minimal damage to the nail plate.

Nail Plate

The nail plate is the hard, keratinized structure made from compact onychocytes, organized in a lamellar pattern. The dorsal surface of the nail plate is smooth with longitudinal ridges. Below the nail plate are the nail bed and part of the nail matrix. The nail bed and nail folds' act as strong attachment points that help the free edge of the nail function as a tool without loosening the nail plate or causing pain.

Nail Bed

The nail bed is attached to the ventral surface of the nail plate and begins distal to the lunular and terminates at the hyponychial. The nail plate is attached to the nail bed through longitudinal epidermal ridges. These ridges on the ventral nail plate surface are complementary to the ridges on the nail bed, which function to increase the surface area of the nail plate's attachment to the underlying nail bed, thus augmenting the adhesion between these two surfaces. The nail bed does not produce a stratum corneum since the keratins necessary for the formation of this layer of the epidermis are not present. However, if onycholysis or loss of the nail plate occurs, the nail bed loses the longitudinal ridges and begins to express the keratins necessary to produce the stratum corneum. Below the nail bed is a thin layer of the collagenous dermis which adheres to the periosteum of the underlying distal phalanx. The lack of subcutaneous fat can increase the risk of osteomyelitis of the distal phalanx in the setting of a nail infection.

Hyponychium
The hyponychium is the area distal to the nail bed and beneath the free edge of the nail plate.

Onychodermal Band
The onychodermal band is part of the distal nail bed that is grossly represented in a contrasting color. It functions as the first barrier of protection on the free edge of the nail and is analogous to the cuticle. Changes in the color can correspond to different diseases or variations in vascular supply.

Nail Art Tools

You already know all about the buffers and clippers and files you need as a manicurist, but nail art brings your tools of the trade to a whole different level. Whether you want to create a fancy French manicure, intricate designs with rhinestones, or a glittery surprise for holiday festivities, here are the seven nail art supplies and tools every manicurist needs to have.

Nail Art Stickers

Nail art stickers come with strong adhesive backing. You should apply them on dry nail polish and seal them with a fast dry topcoat. They come in a variety of designs from flowers to cartoons etc.

Dotting Tools

Dotting tools are a must in your nail art kit. They help in creating dots. They usually come in sets of five with different sizes of 10 heads. They also help in creating some easy nail designs.

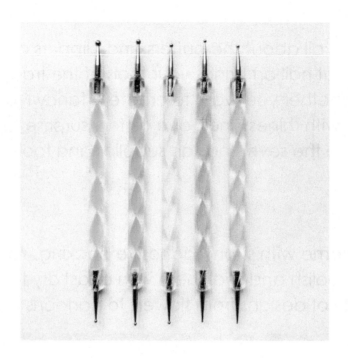

Rhinestones

Acrylic, crystal, or glitter, rhinestones have a charm of their own. Having different colors and sizes or shapes of rhinestones adds that extra bling and style to your nails. Use them to get uniquely designed nails of your desire.

Striping Tapes

These tapes are very thin and help in adding metallic lines in your manicure. These tapes also come in many textures and colors.

Bullion Beads/Sprinkle Beads/Cavier Beads

They are small metal beads or glass beads. These help in creating accent and gives 3D effect to your nails. You can see the Caviar nail art in action.

Loose Glitter

Well, it is not mandatory to have glitter in your nail paint always. You can use loose nail art glitter powder on your nails in your desired quantity for a chic look. You can create flitter french tips by applying topcoat to your nails, then dipping them in glitter pots, removing the excess using a fan brush, and sealing it by applying another layer of topcoat. Also, you can change the look of your tacky nail polish by sprinkling some glitter on top of it using a fan brush.

Nail Polishes

You should have at least some good shades of nail enamels. Don't forget to add black and white shades as they are the most used ones. Also you can add some textured nail enamels or glitter ones. The most trending nail enamel nowadays is magnetic nail enamel.

Nail Stamping Kit

A regular nail stamping kit includes a stamper, a scraper, and a stamping template, but a few can also include stainless steel image plates, clear jelly, and rolls of nail striping tape. The image plates have a plastic backing, making them safe for use, and protecting your nails from the sharp edges.

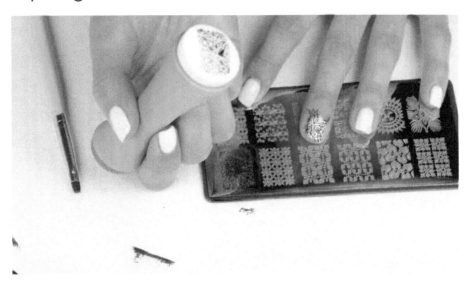

Topcoat and Basecoat

Topcoats and Basecoats are a must-have in your nail art kit. A good top coat not only extends the life of your manicure but also protects your nails and adds shine to them. On the other hand, a base coat protects your nail polish from chipping and yellowing. You can also opt for nail hardening, calcium-based base coats that strengthen your nails.

Orangewood Stick/Toothpick

These are used to pick rhinestones and also help in creating dots. They are also very helpful in water marbling.

Nail Grooming Kit

A nail grooming kit is a must-have in your vanity. It is a multipurpose kit that can be used for manicure, pedicure, facial grooming, etc. This set of 16 tools contains many essentials such as scissors, nail clippers, dead skin pliers, scraping knives, scraping cutters, etc that are useful in creating perfect nail art.

Nail Polish Remover

To remove nail polish, you can try nail polish remover wipes. Kara Nail Polish Remover Wipes are a good option. They are the one-stop solution for pretty nails. The wipes are easy to use and do not contain acetone, toluene, alcohol and paraben. They can easily remove dark shades of nail polishes. They contain natural olive oil and vitamin E. These wipes moisturize your skin as well as prevent peeling of cuticles and chipping of nails, making your nails healthy looking and shiny.

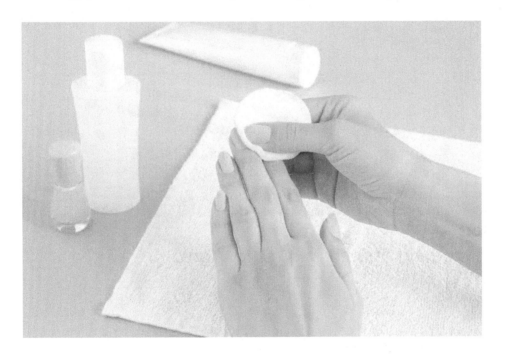

Lint-Free Cotton Swabs/Q-tips

These are needed to clean and remove polish from your nails. Lint-free cotton swabs are important because ordinary cotton may leave cotton fibers on your nails thus ruining your manicure. Q-tip dipped in acetone free remover helps in removing extra polish from cuticles and your manicure looks neater.

Acrylic Colors

They help in creating beautiful nail art designs.

Nail Art Brushes

If you are an ardent nail art lover, having a set of nail art brushes is a must. These brushes help you design your nail art as you desire effortlessly. Each brush has its purpose and designs uniquely like no other. Grab one set and be amazed at its benefits.

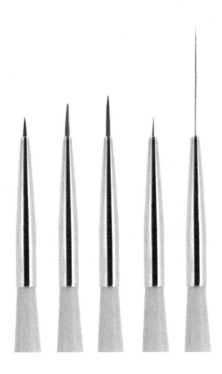

Scissors

Keep scissors on hand for when cutting is needed—while preparing clear sticky tape for stenciling, for example, or cutting lace and other nail decorations.

Tweezers

Tweezers have multiple uses in nail art, primarily acting as an extension of your fingers as you allow wet nails to dry. Use them to pick up tiny decorative crystals and transfer them to the nail, or to remove adhesive strips from the nail with precision.

How to Apply Nail Polish Neatly?

Add a thin layer of petroleum jelly or white school glue around each nail to shield your skin from the polish and create crisp lines.

Wait for each layer of polish to dry before painting on the next one. Aim to use no more than 3 brush strokes per nail.

Remove the petroleum jelly or glue. If there's still polish on your skin, dab an old makeup brush in nail polish remover and wipe along your nail polish line.

Step 1: Preparing Your Nails for Polish

1/Remove old polish from your nails. In order to produce a neat and even manicure, you must first remove any old polish from your nails. Acetone nail polish removers dry out your nail, and cuticle. If possible, use a non-acetone nail polish remover over an acetone nail polish remover.

Place a cotton swab or ball over the opening of your nail polish remover. Make sure it is completely covering the opening of the bottle.

Tip the bottle upside down and wait a few seconds for the cotton swab or ball to become saturated with the remover.

Rub the saturated cotton swab or ball over your nails to remove the polish.

Re-saturate your cotton swab or ball as needed

2/Trim, file and smooth your nails. After removing your old nail polish, devote some time to clipping, shaping and buffing your nails. Locate nail clippers, emery board and a gentle buffer.

Use the clippers to trim your nails, if needed.

Smooth the edges of your nails with an emery board nail file. File your nails into a round, square, or rounded-square shape.

Run over each nail with a slightly abrasive buffer to even out the surface of your nails.

3/Soak your hands in warm water. Once your nails are clipped, shaped, and buffed, take a moment to relax and pamper yourself. Retrieve a basin and fill it with warm water and a squirt of your gentle facial cleanser. Use a gentle body scrub to exfoliate your hands before soaking them. Submerge your hands in the warm, soapy water to remove the body scrub. Soak your hands for three minutes. Remove your hands from the basin and dry them on a clean towel.
After soaking your hands, your cuticles will be soft and easier to push back.
4/Push back your cuticles. Do not do this if it starts really hurting as this could cause them to bleed. It might hurt just a little whilst you do it if you haven't done it for a while. Cuticles are a part of your skin. They protect your nail matrix, the portion of the nail that grows, from infection. Cutting your cuticles leaves your nail matrix open to infections. It can also cause deformities in the nail, such as ridges and discoloration. Instead of cutting your cuticles, push them back to give your nail an oval appearance. It also makes it easier to create a neat polish line.
Use a cuticle pusher to carefully push the cuticle back towards your nail bed.
Push in the sides of the cuticle as well.
Remove any dry or damaged skin.
Repeat on the rest of your nails.

5/Moisturize your cuticles and skin. After exfoliating your hands, it is important to rehydrate and moisturize your soft skin. Select a thick and luxurious hand cream or lotion. Massage this cream or lotion into your hands. Or, apply some almond oil (usually comes in a pen or a nail varnish type pot) or some clearly labeled cuticle oil and apply to your cuticles. This hydrates them and the remaining white half-dead skin will properly get dealt with.

6/Remove oil and grease from your nails. If left on your nails, the oils from your hand cream or lotion will shorten the life of your polish. You can remove these oils from your fingernails with rubbing alcohol and a cotton swab or ball.

Place a cotton swab or ball over the opening of the rubbing alcohol bottle.

Tip the bottle upside down and wait a moment for the cotton swab or ball to become saturated with the rubbing alcohol. Place the bottom of the bottle on a flat surface.

Swipe the rubbing alcohol-saturated cotton swab or ball over your nails to remove the oil.

Repeat as needed.

Step 2: Using Different Tricks to Keep Your Nail Polish Neat

1/Apply a thin layer of petroleum jelly around each nail before painting your nails. Before painting your nails, you can take measures to prevent the polish from drying outside the lines of your nails. You can achieve a perfectly neat mani every time by placing a thin layer of petroleum jelly around the edge of your nail. The oil from the vaseline will serve as a barrier between your skin and the nail polish.

Dab a cotton bud into a jar of petroleum jelly. If you don't have vaseline, you can use lotion.

Swipe the cotton bud around the edges of each nail—keep the cotton bud and petroleum jelly on your skin. Do not let either touch your nail.

Pick out your polish and get ready to paint your nails

2/Apply a thin coat of white school glue around each nail prior to polishing your nails. If you struggle to paint inside the lines of your nails, you can take steps to ensure a swift and neat clean-up. Apply a thin coat of white school glue around the edge of your nails to create a neat, crisp polish line. The glue will protect your skin from the polish.

Dip a cotton bud or brush into a bottle of white school glue.

Use the cotton bud or brush to paint a thin, even layer of white school glue around the edge of each of your nails. Do your best to keep the glue off your nails.

Wait for the glue to dry before you polish your nails.

3/Wait to clean up your nail polish line. As you continue to improve at painting your nails, you may have less errant nail polish to remove from your skin. Instead of applying a thin coat of petroleum jelly or white school glue, you may choose to clean up your nail polish lines after you've finished applying your polish and top coat. You can perfect your polish line with an old makeup brush and nail polish remover. This method requires a steady, practiced hand and patience.
You may also use a clean cotton-bud dipped in nail polish remover.

Step 3: Painting and Drying Your Nails

1/Apply a base coat to each nail and wait for it to dry. Base coats strengthen and protect your nails. This first layer of your manicure also extends the life of your polish. Coat each nail in a thin, even layer of base coat. Allow the base coat to dry.
Swipe the brush on the inside of the bottle's opening to remove excess base coat from the brush.
While you should always use a base coat, it is especially important to use this product if your nails frequently chip, split, or peel. The base coat will help to fortify your nails.
2/Apply the first thin coat of polish in three strokes and allow it to dry. In order to achieve a nice, neat, and even manicure, apply one to three thin layers of polish. You can control the thickness of each coat by only leaving enough polish on your brush to cover one nail. Remove excess polish from your brush by sliding your brush up the inside of the bottle's opening from base to tip. Once you have just enough polish on your brush, apply the paint in three strokes
Place a small dab of polish at the base of your nail above your cuticle. (This prevents the polish from pooling.
Use the brush to pull the dab of polish down towards the cuticle—do your best to leave a small gap of nail between the polish and your cuticle.
Swipe the brush in a straight line from the base to the tip of your nail.
Return the brush to the base of your nail. Move the brush upwards along the left curve of your nail until the entire side is coated in polish.

Return the brush to the base of your nail. Move the brush upwards along the right curve of your nail until the entire side is coated in polish. Repeat this process on each nail.

Allow the polish to dry before adding another coat.

3/Apply a second and/or third thin coat of polish in three strokes and let it dry. As your first coat dries, determine if you need to add a second layer of polish. If your polish is sheer, you may want to add two or more coats; if your polish is opaque, you may not need to add a second and/or third coat. Once your first coat of polish is dry, apply a second coat of polish if desired.

Put a small dot of nail polish at the base of your nail just above your cuticle.

Pull the dot of polish down towards the cuticle with the brush—try to leave a small gap of nail between the polish and your cuticle.

Pull the brush in a straight line from the base to the tip of your nail.

Place the brush at the base of your nail. Swipe the brush along the left curve of your nail until the entire side is coated in polish.

Place the brush at the base of your nail. Pull the brush upwards along the right curve of your nail until the entire side is coated in polish.

Repeat this process on each nail.

Allow the polish to dry before adding a third coat or applying a top coat.

4/Apply an even layer of top coat to each nail and wait for it to dry. Top coat adds a brilliant shine to your polished fingers. Once your nails are completely dry, apply a thin layer of top coat to each nail. If possible, apply a quick-drying top coat to your nails.

Soak your fingernails in ice water to help your polish cure faster.

Step 4: Cleaning Up Your Polished Nails

1/Use a cotton-bud to remove the petroleum jelly from around each nail. If you applied a thin coat of petroleum jelly around the edge of your nails, allow your nails to dry completely before you remove the substance. Once the top coat is dry, trace the edges of your nails with a clean cotton-bud. As you remove the petroleum jelly from your skin, you will also wipe away any polish sitting on top of the oily substance.

2/Peel off the thin coat of glue and excess nail polish from around each nail. When your nails are dry, carefully remove the thin layer of dried white school glue from your skin. As you peel away the dried glue, you will also remove any polish that is outside of your nail polish line. Once removed, you will be left with a neat and crisp nail polish line.

3/Clean up excess polish with an old makeup brush and nail polish remover. After painting your nails, you can carefully remove any excess polish with an old makeup brush dipped in nail polish remover. In addition to a brush a remover, you will also need a cotton swab or ball. When you're done touching up your nail polish lines, you'll be left with a pristine manicure.

Pour out a small amount of nail polish remover into a dish or the bottle's cap.

Dip your brush into the remover and then blot it on a clean cotton swab or ball.

Position the brush next to your untidy nail polish line.

Without applying any pressure, sweep the brush along your nail polish line. Repeat on each nail polish line.

Use the brush to remove nail polish that dried on your skin.

Dip your brush in the remover and wipe your it off on the cotton swab or ball as needed.

False Nails Art

Fake nails — also known as artificial nails — are types of nail extensions that enhance your nails' overall look and aesthetic.

There are a variety of available fake nail styles, designs, and looks. You can go minimalist, festive, chic, seasonal, sultry, spooky, kawaii — literally whatever you want with fake nails.

Whether you want to celebrate individuality, art, or a season or add an oomph to your outfits, we highly recommend getting fake nails.

However, it's important to know beforehand that fake nails have to be maintained to keep them on and to keep them looking fresh.

Nail technicians recommend in-fills for artificial nails every 2 to 3 weeks.

Nevertheless, while fake nail upkeep can be a hassle, they're still here to stay because of their durability and customizability, making them way better than your typical manicure.

Different Types of Fake Nails

1/Acrylic Nails

One of the most popular fake nail types is acrylic nails, which can be applied as a whole nail overlay or a nail tip extension.

Acrylic nails are a combination of a powder polymer and liquid monomer, which creates a paste that is applied to your natural nail.

After applying it and letting it set, the acrylic nails will harden within a few minutes and can then be shaped depending on your preferred shape and length.

Generally, acrylic nails are the most affordable, durable, and thickest of all artificial nail types. Since they don't chip easily, acrylic nails are ideal for active women.

Still, you need to get it touched up after 2 to 3 weeks as your nails grow over time.

Pros:
Affordable
Helps stop chewing habits
Long-lasting

Perfect with poorly structured nails or non-existent nails
Suitable for weak and brittle nails

Cons:
Uses a lot of harsh chemicals
Produces toxic odor and harsh fumes
Can damage your natural nails
Can look fake
Needs to be refilled every month

2/Gel Nails

If you are looking for a nail manicure type that looks natural while protecting your actual nails, you should get gel nails.

Gel nails are made out of gel acrylic, which is hardened with the help of ultraviolet (UV) curing light or an LED nail lamp.

This nail alternative is performed through a 3-step procedure: base coat brushing, nail polish application, and applying top coat on your natural nails.

After every coating, your nails will be put under a UV curing light for about two minutes to dry and cure.

If you are one of those who work with their hands or are active, this nail extension type is not for you because it is not as durable or strong as regular acrylics.

One of the best things about gel nails is that you don't need to have them nail-filled as frequently as acrylic nails.

Also, this fake nail variation has a high-gloss finish and usually lasts longer than regular nail polish.

Pros:
Flexible and feels natural
Quicker to apply
Gentler and safer on nails
Set more quickly
Widely available in colors and patterns

Cons:
More expensive
Needs to be replaced more frequently
Not that durable
Not that long-lasting

3/Dip Powder Nails

Dip powder is a nail styling method that involves dipping the nail into colored powder, which is then sealed on top using a clear sealant. The salon nail technicians now use a brush to apply the dip powder onto the nail for hygienic purposes.
This type of fake nails is a hybrid of acrylic and gel nail polish extensions as it provides the durability of the acrylics and the flexibility of gel nails. With this, you can remain chip-free for up to 4 weeks!
So if you want to save time and get a long-lasting and low-maintenance nail look, dip powder nails will be right up your alley.

Pros:
Easily done at home
Durable
Endless color options
Last up to four weeks
No need to cure with UV lights

Cons:
Sometimes triggers allergies
Looks bulkier compared to nail polish
Non-hygienic in other salons
Removal can be damaging to natural nails

4/Nail Wraps

Nail wraps—also known as polish strips or nail stickers—are designed stickers formed by cutting pieces of materials like silk fabric, linen, or fiberglass to fit on your nail bed. Then, these wraps will be sealed onto your nails with a layer of glue or resin.

These nail stickers can easily be applied at home and be on the go. Getting this nail manicure is perfect if you want instant nail art without spending too much time and money visiting your nearest salon.

However, nail wraps won't be as long-lasting and durable compared to other nail products and fake nails.

Nonetheless, nail wraps are good, especially if you are looking for a budget-friendly and easy DIY option to enhance your nails for any occasion.

Pros:
Effortless nail design
No more mess
Zero dry time

Cons:
Limited creativity
Dries out very quickly
Intensive nail preparation
Possibly damages nails

5/Polygel Nails

If you want a combination of gel and acrylic nail benefits, you should ask your nail technician for a complete set of polygel nails.

Polygel nails are a hybrid nail-enhancement formula that offers you the best gels and acrylic nail features, such as customizability, flexibility, and durability.

Like gel and acrylics, you can use polygel nails to fill in, sculpt, overlay, or even extend your natural nails. Moreover, it is cured under a UV light after application.

Fortunately, this type of fake nail is easy to apply. Even if polygel nails share the same benefits as gels and acrylics, they are a lot lighter than them.

The longevity of these fake nails depends on how well they are applied. Typically, polygel nails can last up to three weeks when properly applied by a certified nail technician.

However, did you know that you can DIY polygel nails in the comfort of your home?

Pros:
Can be easily filed off with a buffer and nail file
Cure fast under a LED light
Flexible and strong
Very light and comfortable to wear

Cons:
Can cause heat spikes when applied incorrectly
Significantly more expensive than other fake nails

Are Fake Nails High Maintenance?

Fake nails require a lot of maintenance. In fact, most fake nail types need users to return to the nail salon every 2-3 weeks to have their nails filled.

If you want to have them stay longer, choose a professional nail technician to get the nail procedure right the first time. That way, you can have your nails properly done, minimizing the risk of nail damage. Also, with the right maintenance and care, you can wait for at least four weeks before you can get them retouched or removed.

Do Fake Nails Damage Your Natural Nails?

Since fake nails can be high-maintenance, you'll need frequent touch-ups to maintain how it looks on your nails. But, know that this can damage your actual nails—eventually making them parched, thin, and brittle.

To prevent that from happening, always listen to your nail tech and follow the nail set schedule to maintain your fake nails and avoid damaging your actual nails.

Also, as much as possible, it would be best to let your nails breathe and have them free from fake nails for some time.

Which Fake Nails Last Longest?

Out of all fake nails, dip powder nails are one of the most long-lasting options because they are comprised of dip powder polymers, which are stronger than those found in gel polish.

Conclusion: Which Fake Nail Should I Get?

Nowadays, various types of fake nails are accessible in the beauty industry. Each of them has pros and cons that you need to weigh.

But, remember, choosing the best artificial nails for yourself is a matter of personal preference.

Regardless of which fake nail type you pick, all you have to do is to maintain them properly to make them look great and avoid damaging your real nails.

DIY NAIL ART PROJECTS

Before you begin a nail art project, you should review the previous sections—Nail Art Tools, Nail Art Techniques, and Nail Anatomy—for expert results and to avoid interruptions and oversights during the projects.

If you're ready. There's no need to wait any longer. LET'S GO!

RAINBOW

Step 01: Prep your nails

Before applying any nail paint, it's essential to prep your nails to ensure that the nail paint goes on smoothly and lasts longer. Start by wiping your nails clean with an acetone-free nail polish remover. It's essential to do this even if you don't have any residue from previously applied polish. Next, cut your nails to the desired length and shape them using a nail file. Clean your nails once again using nail polish remover to get rid of all the dirt from the filing.

Step 02: Apply a base coat

Next, apply a layer of base coat to give the nail paint something to cling on to. This little step will help increase the lifespan of your main. If you don't have a base coat, don't worry. You can even apply a clear nail polish.

Step 03: Add the rainbow dots

After prepping your nails, it's now time to add the color. Pick four to five bright colors, and apply it on the tips. If you don't have the manicure dotting tool, don't worry, you can simply make the dots using either a toothpick, matchstick or a tip.

Step 04: Seal it all in

Once you've applied the colors and are satisfied with how it looks, allow your manicure to completely dry. Once it's dry, apply the top coat and seal everything in. This step will ensure that your manicure stays fresh for a longer period.

Half Moon Manicure

Tool:
a nail file
cuticle oil
Nail polish base
Adhesive hole reinforcement patch
Color nail polish
Tweezers
Clear nail polish
Cotton swab
Nail polish remover

Instructions
1. File your nails into an almond shape
You need to remove the old polish, file your nails into an almond shape.

2. Nourish your nails with cuticle oil

After shaping my nails, I treat them with Cuticle Oil. It comes packaged like a pen with an angled cap and a paintbrush tip. When you twist the pen, oil will secrete at the tip of the pen to brush onto your nails. I use the angled cap to push out my cuticles before applying oil to my nails and cuticles. I let the oil soak in completely before applying nail polish. The store employee told me that almond oil is the only oil that the nails will absorb. I haven't seen the science to back this claim, but the oil seems to soften and nourish my cuticles.

3. Apply a layer of transparent base paint

Now your nails are ready for the first coat of polish. Start by applying a base coat of nail polish, which will help the nail polish last longer. It also protects your nails from staining due to colored paint.

4. Stick the adhesive hole reinforcement patch to create a semicircle

Apply a self-adhesive reinforcement label to the bottom of your nail. I apply them where the inner hole of the sticker fits my cuticle. You can move the stickers up or down depending on how big you want the "moon" to be.

Make sure they're really stuck and won't move around. I also like to press on the edges of the sticker to make sure I can polish up to the edges and so the polish doesn't seep under the sticker.

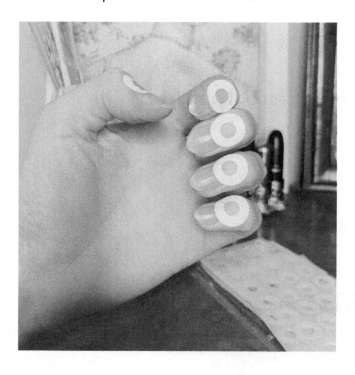

5. Apply two thin coats of color nail polish

Apply two thin coats of nail polish, let the first coat dry before applying the second. This helps the nails dry faster than applying a thicker coat of polish. You can paint right on the sticker. The corners can be a bit tricky, so try to stick as close to the sticker edges as possible.

As for which nail polish color to use, my favorite colors are classic red, magenta or plum. You can use another color like your interest.

6. Remove the reinforcement sticker

Before the second coat of nail polish has completely dried, use tweezers to carefully remove the reinforcement stickers. If you have any stray polish in the half moon, you can use a toothpick to smooth it out or use a cotton swab dipped in nail polish remover.

7. Apply a Clear Top Coat

Once the color nail polish has dried, apply a clear top coat over the entire nail to seal the nail polish. Make sure you wait until the color nail polish is dry or the top coat brush might smudge color polish into the half-moon space as you apply the top coat.

8. Clean Up the Edges

Lastly, use a cotton swap to clean up the edges and any stray polish marks.

Nail Glitter

Tool:
Base coat
Nail polish
Top coat
Loose glitter

Instructions:
Technique #1: All-Over Glitter
Step 1 — Apply a clear base coat. Make sure to apply it evenly so that the glitter will stick to the entire nail!

Step 2 — Dip your nail in the pot of glitter, laying it flat over the surface and rolling it back and forth a bit to cover the sides.

Step 3 — Tap your finger to remove any extra glitter. If you find that the glitter seems chunky or not completely even, you can press it on with your fingers.

Step 4 — As you can see in the picture of my nails above, glitter will probably get on your cuticles. Be sure to wipe it off so the finished product looks precise. I found that an eyeshadow brush is perfect for this, because it dusts all the glitter off without getting it on the fingers of your other hand or messing up your nails.

Technique #2: A Sprinkle of Glitter

Step 1 — Apply a clear base coat and color, as you would with a normal manicure. I used a very pale pink, but colors that are darker or more vibrant would also look awesome.

Step 2 — While the polish is still wet, take a pinch of glitter with your other hand and sprinkle it over the nail.

Step 3 — Tap off the excess and wipe your cuticles clean.

Step 4 — Make sure the nails on one hand are completely dry before doing nails on the other hand. If they're still wet, they will pick up more glitter than you intended to put on them when you go to sprinkle your other nails, and they may start to look messy.

Finishing Up:
Repeat these steps on the rest of your nails. Or don't, and have just a few nails that glimmer. The choice is yours!
After applying glitter, I would recommend at least two top coats to ensure that you get a really good seal and a smooth texture. I used three or four – I like my nails glossy! Be sure to do this gently in order to avoid wiping off chunks of glitter as you go.

Gold Leaf

Tool:
* Nail polish remover
* lint-free wipes or cotton pads
* an orangewood cuticle sticks or cuticle pusher
* 180-grit buffer or a buffing block (the ones with 4 different sides)
* a nail file
* base coat
* two contrasting nail polish colors of your choice
* gold leaf foil
* top coat
* a mini striping brush (small paintbrush or clean eyeliner brush)
* a pair of tweezers
* cuticle oil and hand cream.

Instructions:

1/Begin by removing any old nail polish and then cleanse your nails well with a cotton pad soaked in nail polish remover to remove any natural oils on the nail plate. Don't soak your nails in water before painting them, as they will absorb water and this will compromise your polish, possibly causing it to crack once they start to dry out.

2/Shape your nails to the desired shape with a nail file and brush away any excess dust. Gently push back your cuticles using a cuticle pusher or orangewood stick (orangewood sticks are available from Dollar stores or in beauty section of your local department store) and use the sharp or pointy end to gently remove any cuticle residue left over on the nail.

3/Lightly buff the entire nail surface with a 180 grit buffer (this is usually the rough side on a buffing block). Do not use a nail file as its too rough and it will damage your nail. Brush away any excess dust.

4/If you're using gel polish, skip this next step. A smooth, shiny surface is the perfect canvas for traditional polish, so use the other sides of the buffing block to buff your nails to a shine.

5/Cleanse your nails again with nail polish remover to remove any natural oils that will have come to the surface of the nail. Apply a thin layer of base coat and cure it according to the instructions on your lamp (for gel) or wait for it to dry.

6/Apply a thin coat of your chosen base color (I'm using black) and make sure to cap the free edge (paint along the very tip of your nails). Cure or wait for it to dry.

7/Apply a second, thin coat of your chosen base color and cure or wait for it to dry.

8/Using a mini striping brush, small paintbrush or clean eyeliner brush, dip the brush into your second chosen nail polish color and paint thin, random squiggly lines across your feature nails. Cure or wait for it to dry.

9/Make sure all the doors and windows are closed and slowly open the pot of gold leaf foil. The slightest hint of a breeze will send this stuff flying everywhere! Take the tweezers and gently pull out small pieces of foil and stick them randomly into the sticky inhibition layer of your gel polish. If you're using traditional polish, you'll need to apply a very thin layer of top coat and stick the foil onto that while it's still tacky but not wet.

10/Apply your top coat over the foil (capping the free edges) and cure or wait for it to dry. Finish off your manicure by rubbing cuticle oil onto your nails, cuticles and skin around your nails. Cuticle oil applied daily will nourish your nails and help your polish to last longer by keeping it flexible. Apply hand cream and you're done!

Black Nail Polish with Iridescent Glitter and Shimmer

Tool:

3 g Large Iridescent Glitter Nail Polish

3 g Tiny Iridescent Glitter Nail Polish

1 g Turquoise Shimmer Nail Polish (Sally Hansen Triple Shine Sparkling Water)

1 g Black Nail Polish (Wet and Wild Shine Black)

7 g Suspension Base Coat Nail Polish

Instructions:

1/Begin with your mixing container on a scale and use the tare function to reset to 0.

2/Add 3 grams of the large iridescent glitter polish.

3/Tare the scale and add 3 grams of tiny iridescent glitter polish.

4/Tare the scale and add 1 gram of turquoise shimmer polish.

5/Tare the scale and add 1 gram of black polish.

6/Tare the scale one last time and add 7 grams of suspension base.

7/Mix everything together thoroughly.

After that apply it on your nails as normal. Apply your top coat over and cure or wait for it to dry.

Chain Link

Tool:
oyal blue polish
Gold striper polish
White striper polish
Clear top coat

Instructions:
1/Apply two coats of royal blue polish to all nails and allow to dry after each coat.
2/With the gold striper polish, create chain links by painting connected circles or ovals across the nail. Proceed to the next nail, changing the direction or curve of the chain. Apply to all nails and allow to dry.
3/With the white striper polish, add a white accent to the corner of each chain link by lightly touching the white tip to the nail. Apply to the same corner of each link to give the impression of light reflecting off the chain. Apply to all nails and allow to dry.
4/Apply clear top coat and allow the completed look to dry.

Ombre Nails

Tool:
Base coat (clear nail polish)
White nail polish
Nude or flesh-toned nail polish
Liquid latex tape
Nail polish remover
A small brush or a Q-tip
Disposable makeup sponge
Top coat
* You can replace another color polish

Instructions:
1/Apply The Base Coat
Start with manicured nails. Apply the base coat to protect your nails
and let them dry.
2/Apply The Nude or Flesh-Toned Nail Polish
Apply two coats of nude or flesh-toned nail polish and let it dry.

3/Apply The Liquid Latex Tape to The Cuticles

Apply the liquid latex tape around your nails. It protects the skin from the mess and peels off easily. Wait for it to dry before moving on to the next step.

4/Apply The White Nail Polish to The Sponge

Layer a generous amount of the white nail polish on the tip of the disposable sponge.

5/Apply The Nude or Flesh-Toned Nail Polish to The Sponge

Layer a generous amount of the nude or flesh-toned nail polish below the sponge tip to create a gradient effect.

6/ Dab The Sponge onto The Nail

Hold the sponge so that the white nail polish is at the nail tip and dab it onto your nails.

7/Repeat Steps 5 And 6

Layer some more nail polish on the sponge and stamp it over your nails to get the desired color intensity. Let it dry before moving on to the next step.

8/Remove The Liquid Latex Tape

Peel off the liquid latex tape using a brush or your fingers.

9/Apply The Top Coat

Apply the top coat to smooth out any texture and give your nails a shiny look.

ANOTHER OMBRE STYLE

Step 1: Apply a layer of base coat and allow it to dry.

Step 2: For your base color, apply deep red nail polish.

Step 3: Apply the same red and black nail polish on a sponge. Dab it onto your nails to create an ombre effect.

Step 4: Clean up around the nails.

Step 5: Apply a gel or a matte top coat.

Step 1: Apply the white nail polish as the base coat.

Step 2: Apply the pastel pink and white nail paints on the sponge and dab it onto your nail.

Step 3: Repeat the step to intensify the ombre effect.

Step 4: Apply the silver glitter nail polish to your accent nail.

Step 5: Secure your manicure with a gel finish top coat.

3. Metallic Ombre Nail Design

Step 1: Paint your nails with champagne or gold glitter nail polish and let them dry.

Step 2: Apply liquid latex around the nails.

Step 3: Apply some black and gold polish to your wedge sponge and gently dab it onto the nail edges.

Step 4: Once you are satisfied with the ombre effect, apply a layer of top coat to secure the manicure.

Step 5: Clean up the sides of your nails with a thin brush and some acetone.

Step 1: Apply a base coat to protect your nails.

Step 2: Apply a white base color for the best gradient opacity and allow it to dry.

Step 3: Apply liquid latex around the nails.

Step 4: Apply three stripes of color to your makeup sponge, allowing the colors to overlap slightly.

Step 5: Dab it onto your nail and let the first layer dry. Reapply the colors onto the sponge and repeat the step.

Step 6: Finish off with a top coat to blend the gradient.

Step 7: Peel off the latex. Clear the edges around the cuticles with a brush and acetone.

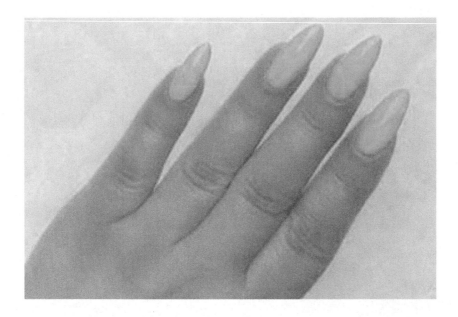

Step 1: Apply a layer of base coat.

Step 2: Apply the first color to one half of your nail.

Step 3: Before the first color dries, apply the second color to the other half of your nail.

Step 4: Take the same two colors with a brush and blend them on a glass base.

Step 5: Apply the blended colors to your nails for a watercolor effect.

Step 6: Finish with a topcoat.

While single-color painted nails have their own charm, an ombre effect adds more pizzazz. You can dial up the effect or tone it down using muted or vibrant shades to reflect your current mood. Think of your nails as your canvas and let your creativity take over. Get your polishes out and create nail art that's nothing short of a masterpiece.

Negative Space

Tool:
Scissors
Sticky tape (preferably masking tape)
Tweezers
Black polish
Angled-edge eyeliner brush (optional)
Nail polish remover (optional)
Paper towel (optional)
Clear top coat

Instructions:
1/With scissors, cut ten pieces of masking tape. Each piece should be slightly longer than the width of your nail, and ⅛ in/4 mm wide. Lightly stick pieces to the edge of a table surface until needed.
2/With tweezers, pick up one piece of tape at a time and place a strip horizontally across the middle of each unpainted nail. Press firmly, and use tweezers to press tape into the edges where the nail meets the cuticles.

3/Apply black polish to all nails, painting the bottom half and then the top half, using upward strokes. Take care along the edges of the tape so polish does not leak under the tape. Allow to dry, then apply a second coat.

4/When polish is completely dry, use tweezers to remove the strips of tape, pulling slowly and carefully from one side to another.

5/If polish has leaked under the tape, leaving behind a jagged line, dip the angled-edge eyeliner brush into polish remover, press against a paper towel to soak up excess, and apply the bristles to the area for precise cleanup.

6/ Apply clear top coat and allow the completed look to dry.

Leopard

Tool:

Light brown gel polish – Butterscotch
Dark brown gel polish – Firewood
Bronze glitter gel polish – Bronze Medallion
Black gel polish – Serious Black
Nail art brush
Ultra Fine Detail Brush
Urban Graffiti Top Coat

Instructions:

1/Apply your base coat

To begin your leopard print nails, start by applying your base color. We've used Urban Graffiti Butterscotch gel polish for our base because it's a perfect beige-brown tone for this look and light enough to apply other colors on top of. Simply apply two coats and cure your nails under your light when finished (LED for 30 seconds or U.V for 120 seconds).

2/Create your leopard spots

Next, take your second, darker color (Firewood), and start to add your leopard spots with your nail art brush. The great thing about these freehand leopard print nails is that they don't need to be perfect! Just remember to add your spots across the nail in irregular shapes, varying them in size, so they don't look too uniform. When finished, cure them again under your lamp.

3/Add your third color

Once you're happy with your leopard print spots, you can add your third, sparkly gel polish color (Bronze Medallion), which will create a lovely two-tone effect and a gorgeous glittery finish. Simply take your brush and lightly dot the glittery color in the center of each brown spot. Try not to make them too circular; they need to look like leopard print rather than polka-dots. When you're finished, cure them again.

4/Define the spots

Next, take your finger nail art brush and your black gel color (Serious Black). Using small strokes, lightly add a little black polish around your leopard print spots, making the top and the bottom of each spot thickest. This will add the final touches to your leopard print nails and give them a more realistic, leopard-like look. Again, they don't all have to look the same! The beauty of this design is they don't need to be too precise. Just slowly add the black to each spot until you're happy with your leopard print design, and then cure them again.

5/Add a top coat

And finally, to finish your leopard nails, add your top coat to give them a gorgeously glossy finish. You can use a matte top coat if you prefer, but the gloss will help enhance the glitter on your spots. Once you've applied the top coat, cure your nails one final time and finish the whole thing with a dab of cuticle oil on each nail.

Mosaic

Tool:
Red polish
Maroon polish
Pink polish
Blue polish
Gold glitter
Striper polish
Clear top coat

Instructions:
1/Apply one coat of red polish to all nails and allow to dry.

2/Apply maroon polish to the nail in angular shapes. For example, paint one corner of the nail maroon, or add a maroon triangle to one side of the nail. Make every nail look different by getting creative with maroon color placement. (Don't worry if edges are uneven; you will soon outline the shapes in gold glitter striper polish.) Apply to all nails and allow to dry, then apply a second coat if denser color coverage is needed and allow to dry.

3/Apply pink polish wherever you like, in complementary angular shapes as you did with the maroon polish. Apply to all nails and allow to dry.

4/Repeat step 3, applying blue polish in complementary angular shapes and allow to dry.

5/With the gold glitter striper polish, paint lines where the different colors meet, applying light, even strokes. Repeat until you are happy with the density of the glitter, allowing time to dry in between coats.

6/When dry, apply clear top coat and allow the completed look to dry.

Glitter Studs

Tool:
Black glitter
Pink polish
Clear top coat
Disposable white plastic plate
Double-sided dotting tool (or toothpick)

Instructions:
1/Sprinkle a pinch of black glitter on your workspace for easy access.

2/Apply one coat of pink polish to all nails and allow time to dry.

3/While allowing pink polish to dry, pour a pea-sized drop of clear top coat on the plastic plate.

4/Apply a second coat of pink to one nail and allow it to dry for 60 seconds. The slightly wet polish will act as an adhesive for the glitter. Apply a second coat of pink to one nail and allow it to dry for 60 seconds. The slightly wet polish will act as an adhesive for the glitter.

5/Dip the small end of the dotting tool into the puddle of clear top coat, then lightly touch it to a single piece of glitter. The glitter will adhere to the tip of the dotting tool for easy transfer to the nail. Position the dotting tool directly above the nail surface, wherever you want to apply the piece of glitter. Place the first piece of glitter in the center of the nail. Gently press the dotting tool to the nail and then lift off, leaving the glitter attached to the nail. (If using a toothpick instead of a dotting tool, slightly moisten the end and use it to pick up individual pieces of glitter, then apply to the nail as described above.)

6/Repeat step 5, applying glitter above and below the center piece, leaving even amounts of space between each piece and creating a neat dotted line down the nail. Add dotted lines to either side, shifting the placement slightly to create a staggered design.

7/Proceed to the next nail, repeating steps 4 to 6 until all nails are complete. If the puddle of top coat dries so that it does not adhere to the dotting tool, simply pour a fresh pea-size puddle.

8/When dry, apply clear top coat and allow the completed look to dry.

Cubic

Tool:
Light pink polish
Light blue polish
Red polish
Black polish
Clear top coat

Instructions:
1/Apply two coats of light pink polish to all nails and allow to dry after each coat.

2/aint the right half of each nail with light blue polish, using a steady hand to create a smooth, even line from the bottom to the top of the nail. Allow to dry and apply a second coat if stronger coverage is needed.

3/With red polish, paint the top right corner of each nail, using the flat edge of the brush to create straight lines. (Don't worry if you get polish outside the nail; you can clean up later.) Allow to dry, then apply a second coat if needed.

4/With the black polish, paint the top left corner of each nail. Allow to dry, then apply a second coat if needed.

5/When dry, apply clear top coat and allow the completed look to dry.

Decals nails

Tool:
A glass of water
Tweezers
Fast-drying top coat
Full nail water slide stickers/decals

Instructions:
1/First take the decal according to your nail size and trim it if needed.

2/Now take the decals and dip them in a glass of water with help of tweezers.

3/After a few seconds, take that out and it will slide automatically from its backing

4/Now put the decal on your nail and press them according to its shape

5/Cut the excess and smooth down the decal using the emery board given in the pack.

6/Finally, apply a fast-drying top coat, and you are done. But keep one thing in mind that you should be doing one nail at a time.

Galaxy nails

Tool:
Black polish
Blue, plum, white, turquoise, and silver sparkle acrylic paint (or you can use nail polish)
Top coat (this one is a cult favorite)
Makeup sponge
Toothpicks

Instructions:
1/Apply 1-2 coats of black polish to your nails and let dry.

2/Pour out a little bit of each of your acrylic colors on a plate. Taking a makeup sponge, start with the white and lightly sponge on a bit of white. Follow up with a little bit of the royal blue and purple. Play around with the sponging until you like the look.

To add more dimension, add just a tiny bit of white over the top with your sponge. Make sure you leave some of the black polish showing around your nails for added depth. Finally, take a little bit of the silver sparkle.

I know it's tempting, but just add a teeny tiny amount of sparkle. It ends up taking away from the look too much if it's too sparkly.

3/Using a toothpick, add little dots on your nails to represent stars. I even made a slightly bigger star on each by drawing a tiny cross with the toothpick.

4/Seal the deal with a top coat. This brings everything together and gives a nice shine to the look. Don't forget this step. Makes a huge difference in the final look and keeps your main from chipping.

Gold Star Manicure

Tool:
Gold star confetti
Wax pencil
Clear top coat

Instructions:
1/Start with clean nails that have been trimmed and shaped to your liking (this is a great all-purpose manicure set to have around).

2/Spread out a few of your star confetti so they are easy to get to. Put a moderately thick coat of clear polish on one finger.

3/Quickly use your wax pencil to pick up stars one at a time and place them on the wet polish. Keep placing stars until you like the overall pattern.

4/Repeat the process with each nail until all your nails have stars. Allow the clear coat to totally dry, and then use two more coats of polish overtop to seal in the design with dry time between each coat. Once your nails are dry, add a coat of cuticle oil to keep your nails healthy.

Holograph Foil Manicure

Tool:
Nail foils
Nail foil adhesive
Base coat color nail polish
Top coat (it's better not to use a quick dry top coat for this)
Cuticle stick
Small pair of scissors

Instructions:
1/Cut and trim your nails to desired shape and apply a few coats of whichever base coat you would prefer. I chose to use a white polish so the pink foil would clearly stand out against it.

2/Once your nails are totally dry, use your scissors to cut triangle strips from your nail foil paper that are about 3/4" long (you can cut one that's a little smaller for your pinky).

3/Cut some straight and long but thin strips of foil as well if you want to do little stripes next to your triangle pieces.

4/Brush a thin but even coat of foil adhesive over your nails and let them dry (I would do one hand at a time). The glue should turn clear when dry, but you really don't want it to be too wet or the foil won't stick. So, I would wait about 15-20 minutes to make sure it's dry enough. It should be a little tacky, but not wet.

5/When the glue is dry enough, place a piece of your foil where you want to apply it to your nail and use your orange stick to rub the foil onto the nail so the pattern will transfer to the tacky glue beneath. You'll want to rub pretty hard to get it to stay, but you can always lift up a bit on the end that's hanging over the edge of your nail to see what's sticking and what's not.
Once your foil is fully rubbed onto the nail, peel the rest of the transfer strip off the nail and it should leave the foil design behind!
Repeat with each nail until you have your shape on each one.
You can either leave just your triangle shapes, or you can add some long thin strips next to the shapes for more of a pattern. Just apply onto the glue, rub, and peel the transfer layer off!

6/Seal your foil with a quick coat of top coat (they recommended not doing multiple passes if you can help it to keep the foil intact), and once your top coat is dry.

Gel Pens Nails

Tool:
Gel pens

Instructions:
Gel pens work very well to draw designs directly onto the nail. And until they are sealed with top coat, the nail can be wiped off — making it easy to start over if you make a mistake. For this manicure, I used gel pens in neon colors (Gelly Roll pens) to create a striped pattern on each nail.

1/Crystal ball

Apply two layers of a Blue-sky white gel polish of your choice and cure it for 60 seconds in an LED lamp/2 minutes in UV.

Apply our no wipe matte top coat and cure for 60 secs in LED/2 min in UV. Tip: if you choose to apply a top coat with a sticky layer, make sure you wipe it with cleanser and wait for 30-60 secs so that you're able to control the ink from the Aqua Color pen.

Apply 2-3 drops of Blue-sky Aqua Color pen number 4 and 2-3 drops of number 5.

Get your brush that is lightly dipped in Cleanser solution and spread the colors to blend. Wait 30-60 secs and let it dry naturally – there's no need to cure it.

Apply no wipe top coat and cure for 60 secs in an LED lamp/2 mines in UV.

2/Flower power

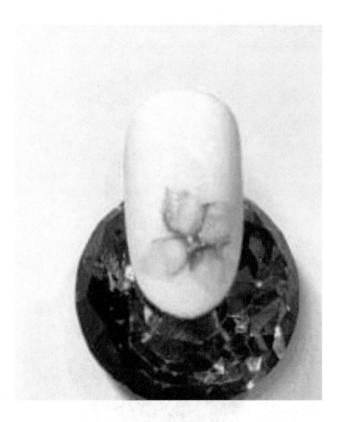

Apply two layers of a Blue-sky white gel polish of your choice and cure it for 60 secs in an LED lamp/2 mines in UV.

Apply our no wipe matte top coat and cure for 60 secs in LED/2 min in UV. As with look one, if you choose to apply a top coat with a sticky layer, make sure you wipe it with cleanser and wait for 30-60 secs so that you're able to control the pen's ink.

Use Aqua Color pen number 5 and apply two small dots opposite each other towards the right corner of the nail.

With your brush, pull the color to make it shear. Let it dry naturally for 30 secs.

Once dry, apply another two drops in between the first two and repeat step four to turn it into a petal.

Finish with a no wipe top coat and cure for 60 secs LED/2 min UV.

3/ Spring vibes

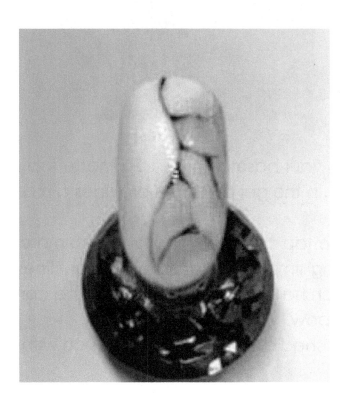

Choose your favorite Blue-sky white gel polish and apply two layers; cure for 60 secs in an LED lamp/2 mines in UV.

Apply our no wipe matte top coat and cure for 60 secs in LED/2 min in UV.

Apply 2-3 drops of Aqua Color pen number 3 and number 4.

Add in 2-3 drops of number 5 in the gaps as shown.

Get your brush and carefully blend the colors together. Wait 30-60 seconds to let it try naturally. If you need more cleanser to blend, then just re-apply to your brush.

Apply a no wipe top coat and cure for 60 secs LED/2 min UV.

Finally, use our black gel paint with a thin liner brush to outline the patterns and cure.

4/Rainbow Style

Start by applying your base color. Add a matte top coat before you begin drawing with the gel pens. This provides a nice surface for the gel ink to grip onto.

2 Once the matte top coat is dry you can begin drawing your designs. I stuck to something simple and just drew straight lines in different directions on each nail, beginning with pink and continuing through the colors of the rainbow.

When you are finished drawing, seal the design with top coat.

Crystals (Gems)

Tool:
 nail crystals
 Scissors
 Sticky tape
 Tweezers
 polish
 Clear top coat
 Disposable white plastic plate
 Nail glue
 Double-sided dotting tool (optional)

Instructions:
1/ Prep the nail and then apply two coats of gel polish, curing after each.

2/Use a lint-free wipe soaked with cleanser to remove the tacky layer, but do not apply to coat. Lightly buff the base of the nail.

3/Place a dab of gel adhesive on the buffed area of the nail.

4/Using a pointed wax pen, pick up a large pointed-back gem, then place it on the gel adhesive at an angle. Repeat this step for additional gems, then cure the nail.

5/ Apply resin between and around the gaps of the larger gems. For better adhesion, spray gems with an aerosol nail drying spray.

Plaid

Tool:
Yellow polish
Light gray polish
Dark gray striper polish
Black striper polish
Clear top coat

Instructions:
1/ Apply two coats of yellow polish to all nails and allow to dry after each coat.

2/With the light gray polish, paint two vertical lines and two horizontal lines, creating an evenly spaced grid. Apply to all nails and allow to dry.

3/With the dark gray striper polish, fill in the squares where the vertical and horizontal lines intersect. Apply to all nails and allow to dry.

4/With the dark gray striper polish, paint a thin line down the center of each vertical and horizontal line. Apply to all nails and allow to dry.

5/ With the black striper polish, paint a plus sign (+) in the middle of each gray square. Apply to all nails and allow to dry.

6/Apply clear top coat and allow the completed look to dry.

Brick

Tool:
Cream polish
Brick red striper polish
Clear top coat

Instructions:
1/ Apply two coats of cream polish to all nails and allow to dry after each coat.

2/With the brick red striper polish, paint two equal-size horizontal rectangles at the midline of the nail.

3/Directly above and below the midline, paint new lines of rectangles— three per row or one long rectangle—to create a staggered look.

4/Continue adding staggered rows of rectangles until the nail is covered with brick pattern.

5/ Proceed to the next nail and continue until all nails feature the design.

6/When dry, apply clear top coat and allow the completed look to dry.

Fake nails

Tool:
Nail polish remover with acetone (the conditioning agents in acetone-free formulas can affect proper adhesion)
Cotton pads
Q-tips
Orange stick
Pack of nails
Nail buffer
Nail file
Glue (Use nail glue only)
Scissors (In case you need to cut back the top of the glue)

Instructions:
1/ Clip Your Natural Nails
Clip your natural nails down close to the fingertips. Keeping a short shape won't interfere with the artificial nails you're about to apply.

Then, very gently push your cuticles back using an orange stick. If your cuticles are sensitive, be sure to push them back slowly. Going too fast can cut them, and then you won't be able to continue applying the artificial nails.

After pushing back your cuticles, buff the surface of your natural nails to roughen them—this makes the fake nails adhere better. Note that buffers come in a range of grit numbers, with the lower numbers being coarser; Saunders recommends using a buffer with no more than 180 grit to shape and finish.

2/Choose Your Nail Size
Press-on nails come in different sizes, and finding the right fit will ensure your nails look natural and last. If they're too small, they may lift and come off prematurely. So in case you're in between sizes, it's best to size up. Press the fake nail against your real nail to ensure it fits. "Your natural nail shouldn't be exposed," says Grant. Then, file your press-on nails until the edges line up with the edges of your natural nails.

3/Apply Glue
Put a dot of glue on the fake nail and one on the real nail—try to avoid over-gluing. A small drop is all you need because it will expand once it hits a flat surface. While nail adhesives are an option, Saunders does not recommend them because they are less durable.

4/Press On Nails
Place the fake nail just above the cuticle (keep it straight as you don't want any crooked-looking nails) and then press down onto the nail bed. Saunders says to press with the orange stick instead of your finger or nails so that they won't get glued together.

Keep pressure applied for 10 seconds to ensure no air bubbles are present before you move on to the next nail. This step is essential because if the fake nail is not secured to the nail bed, moisture may get underneath and cause lifting or nail fungus.

5/ Finishing Touches

After your nails have been applied, take a Q-tip and wipe around the cuticle to pick up any glue that has seeped out from under the fake nail. Then, if you so choose, take a nail file and file down your set to your preferred length.

Keep the top of the nail glue as clean as you can (remember, if you wipe it with soft tissue, the tissue will stick), and keep the bottle upright so you can reuse it.

Made in the USA
Las Vegas, NV
29 December 2024

15542134R00057